ADVANCE PRAISE FOR *JONAHWHALE*

'The poems in Ranjit Hoskote's *Jonahwhale* are brilliant annotations on the giant landmass of history. With wisdom and erudition in plenty and a masterly grip on the quiet but lethal drama of verse, *Jonahwhale* is, on any measure, a major achievement.'—George Szirtes, poet and translator; author of *The Burning of the Books* and *Bad Machine*

'A wonderfully ambitious, sophisticated and charged collection: a symphony of the sea in three great movements. The first explores history, language, geography, the Indian Ocean and colonization, with Shakespearian echoes of *The Tempest*. Then comes contemporary and personal human "traffic" – and urban alienation; and the third delves deeply into art. The forms, exquisite lyrics, philosophical insights, prose poems, epics with still moments of pure simplicity, are as multiple and shape-shifting as water. An astonishing achievement.'—Ruth Padel, professor of poetry, King's College, London; author of *Darwin: A Life in Poems* and *The Mara Crossing*

'What is each poem in the world but a speck of land lost upon the ocean of language itself? We must then navigate ourselves through poets like Ranjit Hoskote and books like *Jonahwhale*. As ever before, through his imagistic, complex, dazzling poems, Hoskote's grand grounded intelligence, and the width of his learning, comes concentrated into brilliant meditations on what poetry can do when reflecting upon an essential theme of human culture. For, reading *Jonahwhale*, it is clear to any reader the poet's name is Ocean, and these poems are both the water and the sea creatures, with this book as our raft.'—S.J. Fowler, poetry editor, *3:AM Magazine*; lecturer in creative writing at Kingston University; curator, 'The Enemies Project'

'Epic in scale, yet written with curatorial precision, *Jonahwhale* is Ranjit Hoskote's magnum opus. Here is a poet with extraordinary sensory awareness – especially hearing and sight/vision – who applies a poetics/ poethics of listening, one that is consistently generous and open to the world, therefore truly of the world. Linguistically innovative, but always social and ethical, these poems are, above all, sensitive to the precariousness of human knowledge and existence. The whale evades capture as we stand "on this narrow island of what we know" (or presume we know). Ranjit is one of the great connoisseurs of English language poetry, someone who holds up each word before him with the care of a jeweller. His mastery of form and lineation is constantly impressive (read the long-form poems like "Cargo and Ballast" and "Poona Traffic Shots" amid several short lyric poems, many dedicated to others). Poems like these reappropriate the love poem in an age often lacking friendship and compassion. *Jonahwhale* is an essential and humbling reaction to the world we live in and it should be read widely.'—James Byrne, editor, *Wolf*; author of *Everything Broken Up Dances*

Jonahwhale

Jonahwhale

RANJIT HOSKOTE

For Ranjani,
in warm friendship — and
thinking back to our reading
in Hyderabad. Very best wishes,
Ranjit
19 Jan 2018
Bandra

PENGUIN

An imprint of Penguin Random House

HAMISH HAMILTON

USA | Canada | UK | Ireland | Australia
New Zealand | India | South Africa | China

Hamish Hamilton is part of the Penguin Random House group of companies
whose addresses can be found at global.penguinrandomhouse.com

Published by Penguin Random House India Pvt. Ltd
7th Floor, Infinity Tower C, DLF Cyber City,
Gurgaon 122 002, Haryana, India

Penguin
Random House
India

First published in Hamish Hamilton by Penguin Random House India 2018

10 9 8 7 6 5 4 3 2 1

ISBN 9780670090235

Typeset in Adobe Caslon Pro by Manipal Digital Systems, Manipal
Printed at Replika Press Pvt. Ltd, India

www.penguin.co.in

In memory of Chandra Hoskote (1934–2015),
my mother, my first reader

the great fish glides through the river
    touching the near bank
                and the far
    the self swims the currents
        of dream
            and waking

—*Brihadaranyaka Upanishad* (4.3.18)

Contents

I. MEMOIRS OF THE JONAHWHALE

I

MEMOIRS OF THE JONAHWHALE

The Churchgate Gazette

I.

Last word on the subject, I promise.
I walked into the train station and it was terrifying.
Like nerve gas had laid the architecture out flat,
the tall glass columns bloodshot and the booking clerks
slumped over, all dead at the till.

A plaster Gandhi with sulphur-rimmed eyes
stopped me (what a substitute for kohl and *why?*).
You missed the last train, it said, he said,
you missed the last and only train that was safe
for a man who's left half his life behind.

II.

A straggler from a late-night movie had more advice.
You could so easily gag on a wine-red, tasselled silk scarf
stuffed in your mouth, he said, you could so easily gag
on sour saliva or a shard of bay leaf
or a letter swallowed just after the bell has rung
and before the door opens.

III.

I thought of the possibilities as I left the station without a
    compass.
Walk straight enough, said Gandhi, and you could walk into
    the sea.
At the wharf, the sailors' wives were keening together:
they were singing the last songs of the whales.
I was their brother and I had killed them
with my broken harpoon and my rusted smile.

IV.

Find affection, I told myself. That's fundamental.
Find a voice that doesn't draw blood
each time you hear it. I walked past myself,
I rippled across lean men and sleek women
laughing behind plate glass, their hands caught
in pools of light, wine gleaming in brittle flutes.

V.

Birdsong disturbs the king of incomplete lives.
He wakes up in the middle of the novel he's writing
in the Midnight Hotel. His eyes need shielding
from the raw clarity of neon. He is back
where he began, with a plate of waxy grapes
and a blunt silver knife on his bedside table.

VI.

Break, ice, for me.
Let me fall through stinging water
in my skin of rust and flame.

I've jumped from a tree
that's branched into the clouds.
It's sucked up all the reality

I've watered it with.
Its fruits are red and wrinkled.
I plunge into drowned gardens

where I walked once.
Sinking, the water stroking
my crown of leaves

as it comes apart,
dark tribune, archaic clown,
I open my eyes.

The Map Seller

for Nikola Madzirov

The roof's dripping with pigeons and I've just escaped
the worst of the sun, strapped on my scuffed leather bag,
and in a moment – this shade's delicious – and before
the pedlars start shouting, *Say your piece! Say your piece!*
I'll start calling out names and pulling countries from it:
big countries, small countries, countries broken in two,
countries the size of handkerchiefs and countries engorged
with other countries, buffer zones jostled by failed states,
island republics sinking by degrees. Even nuclear powers
that started as papaya plots or guano archipelagos.
Whatever you like, I've got a map that looks like it –
and you can have any piece of my flaking jigsaw atlas,
if only I could reach you across this accordion sky
that's billowed open to rain on all the hats I wear:
tribune of nowhere, midnight's newscaster,
out-of-work weatherman, all-terrain refugee.
And across this trench that a JCB's dug along my street:
tomorrow's avenue, today's wide sludge grave.

The Atlas of Lost Beliefs

Without waking up, turn to page thirty-seven
in the *Atlas of Lost Beliefs*
and surround yourself

with apsaras, kinnaras, gandharvas, maenads,
satyrs, sorcerers, bonobos, organ grinders,
stargazers, gunsmiths, long-distance runners,
gravediggers, calligraphers, solitary reapers,
beenkars, troubadours, rababias, ronin,
nagas, pearl divers, Vandals, Goths,
mummers, snipers, collectors of moths,
hobos, dharma bums, bauls, drifters,
djinns, mahjubs, marabouts, qalandars,
griots, mad hatters, speakers in tongues,
trippers, star angels, batmen, punks,
eggheads, buffoons, lay preachers, agitators,
friends of the court, friars minorite, agents provocateurs,
bird-spangled shamans, fainting oracles, screeching owls,
wise men of Gotham, and women who run with wolves

all blessed by the blue hand of a reckless dancer
who spares a thought or two for the world but no more
as she poses, heels in the air, Cossack-kicking on a crumbling
    reef.

Seven Islands

sand-wrought storm-humped

                                these islands

                never complain

                                they take what comes

craft

        one name for seven

from dropped iron   lost rivers and

        spits of reclaimed   land starved

                        ocean

        wind-ripped   light-riveted

        gravel-spun   overrun

        roads that take you

        to where   step by step

                                        the water is

                                        sweet and deep

the only way up

                until help arrives

                                                is south

Ocean

my name is Ocean
    I shall not be contained
        my tides spell
        starting gun and finish line
afterwards only shells
          and scattered roofs
will remind you I was
            there
my combers wash away the roots of trees, towns, the shaken heart
    but mortals there's hope
              my breakers hurl seeds back at your shores
    after the flood the chroniclers will write
           in Konkani, Sabir, Aymara, Tulu, Jarawa,
           Krio, Tok Pisin:
           after the flood the beach exploded with giant
           peacock trees
in whose branches on windy days you could hear
the surge
and swell
        of Ocean summoning whales, whalers who chased
        blood-wakes,
        red-haired women who fought pirates, sleepless
        harpooners
        who sailed from fjordlands to where
              volcanoes splintered the sleeping ice,

furies who choked pearl divers, drove catamarans
aground,
voyagers who fell into the sea and grew wings
        Ocean reciting from his depths
every drifting epic of pursuit, every song of shipwreck,
every trace of raft and sail and trailing anchor
flotsam   jetsam   buckram   vellum
                          he could remember

Ahab

Captain of castaways, the pilot calls out and his curse carries
                       across docks, derricks, opium factories:
                       a typhoon in the horse latitudes.
He's hurled his ship after the whale
that swallowed him and spat him out.
                       The monster is the only system he's known.
At the bridge, he's drenched in the dark:
locked on target, silent, furrowed,
Saturned to stone.

*

Across steep tides, through walls of water, his life has always
      been pursuit.
                       As the ship splinters on the reef,
                       the rigging becomes his noose.
Brine blistering his throat, he thinks:
                       If only I'd harpooned this monster on a page.

Spelling the Tide

We drew near the island, the surf a cannonade on its stony
    beaches,
no landing.
We dropped anchor.
Some fishermen came down
     to the water's edge and called out. We called back.
The surf roared in our ears, no one
                  heard no one.
The skirling wind shredded our voices and danced on them.
We pointed
        at the canoes
they'd hauled out of tide's reach.
Come get us.
They didn't get us
        or didn't want to.
We made signs.
The skirling wind shredded our signs and danced on them.
       They melted away in the rain.
Water in your sails, shirts, socks is wet lead.
Prayer in that storm
        was just a mouth gone wrong.
We tried our hands instead.
We made all
     the signs we knew.
The skirling wind shredded our sails and danced on them.

Cape Caution

When you're swimming from Cape Caution to Impulse Bay,
don't miss the line where jade touches turquoise and recoils:
this is the jolt where nerve end meets salt,
this is the neverskin,
this is where you grow knife-edged fins and plunge:

you're one light tremor away from sabre teeth.

The Heart Fixes on Nothing

Zafar

The heart fixes on nothing in this wasted province.
Whoever made anything of a kingdom of shadows?

Go find another home, my smothered hopes.
This stained heart has no roof to offer you.

I prayed for long life and got four days:
two were spent in desire, two in waiting.

Gardener, don't rip these thorns from the garden:
they were raised with the roses by a gentle spring.

The nightingale doesn't blame the gardener or the hunter:
Fate had decided spring would be its cage.

Fate's real dupe: that would be you, Zafar, your body denied
two yards of spaded earth in the Loved One's country.

And Sometimes Rivers

And sometimes rivers
that run in your veins
change course.
Silt marks the spot
from where you set sail
to circumnavigate the globe
and where someone wearing your sunburned face
stopped thrashing about in mangroves that wouldn't let go
and stood still, bleached hair ruffled by the wind,
as if, after a voyage charted across fevers and hurricanes,
riding at anchor.

Risk

The earth here is glass, the wind the sting of a thousand wasps.
Whoever is driven north wishes he could burn in the fires
   of hell.
On this sea without horizons we do not sail by the magnet.
Of wisdom, the deep says, 'It is not in me.'

As It Emptieth It Selfe

I.

At the mouth of the dog river
    foam words foam words
    currents of sand arrowing after fog birds
slack shadows engraved on the veil of the tide
      that shimmers in and sags out
for the twentieth the thirtieth the emptieth time
the river going with the sea the sea going homewards
As It Emptieth It Selfe

You shall build your citadels on silt said the preacher
    and sink your pride in spice currents
    take your parakeets and painted cormorants
with you but leave the coconut palms and the Inca silver
    leave behind a bloodful of curses
with strands of indigo wet bales of cotton
on this parched delta these dragged fields of salt
sweet strained with brack
For the Emptieth Time

II.

Splayed in his planter's chair, the saboteur of silences toys
with a breech-loading Bible, cocked in defiance of treaties.

17

Nib sharpened by monsoon hungers, the chronic ache
of working in a country without plums or Bordeaux,
he writes home:

In this damnable climate, steel rusts, razors lose their edge.
Thread decays, clothes fall to pieces. Books moulder away.
Plaster cracks, timber rots,
the matting hangs in shreds. Fungus inscribes itself
on vellum bindings as the tattoo of rain on the roof
drowns out the mind's arias.

The clouded mirror's been my only proper companion
since Ovid and Seneca fell apart.
I've been reading palmleaf manuscripts with sour pandits
and picking up opium and Tamil from sallow lascars
in this pidgin district, waiting for the mailboat
to bring me the necessities:
sherry, walnuts, Trichinopoly cigars.

I have hidden in the houses of the bibis who breed
our scabby byblows, who run around the gullies
with their tow hair and improbable grey eyes:
their fortunes will be the fortunes of Homer's sailors.
Before they indenture themselves
to war or shipwreck or sirens or mutiny,
we'll tame the little devils, give them Greek
or Irish names, teach them a respectable tongue.

Then we'll lop them off the family tree
and send them out on battered frigates
to fight and die for King and Country.

III.

Try mangrove instead of watercress.
Try chameleons instead of retrievers.
The earth webs your feet here, and look out
for rivers that bite.

Stone in the veins.

This country smelted from copper
and scented with mustard
has secret names that only
its lovers can nose out.

IV.

The river stabs the sea.
Water, salt and fresh, bursts up
through the splintered ribs of the scuttled boat
that's trailed a wake of belly-up fish.
Thalassa. The compass bird points to the coast:
to a rivermouth disgorging crumbled islands,
to the tidewash that numbs the wounds
by which conquerors named it.
Trapped by the trader's sovereign eye,
by the surveyors of revenue lands,
the purveyors of clove and camphor,
the coast signals its own tongue:

breaking with the horizon's grammar,
a stutterance.

Lascar

Bombay–Liverpool–London, 1889

The lascar was always sallow. It didn't help
that his name anagrammed rascal. He carried
a whiff of scurvy, a hint of rats in the hold,
hulls battered by typhoons.
He was never far from dirty work.
Here's what the detective said:
There's a trapdoor at the back of that opium den,
near the wharf, which could tell strange tales
of what passes through it on moonless nights.
Here's what the good wife said:
At the foot of the stairs I met this lascar,
who thrust me back and, aided by a Dane,
pushed me out into the street.
Meanwhile her husband:
Only one man knew my secret. He was the keeper
of a low den in which I used to lodge.
A lascar, well paid by me for his rooms,
my secret was safe with him.
Neither detective nor wife nor husband knew
the bleached village on the Konkan coast,
or had seen the forced parades at tropical noon,
the forts locked in rising silt, the standing crops burned.

History gave you one name. Fear
gave you and your cousins others.
To novelists: Savage.
To pamphleteers: Cannibal.
To scholars: Anthropophage.
To your captains: Seacunny, tindal,
syrang, topaze. Or mostly
as you swabbed the deck:
Cocoa-faced rascal!

You call yourself names
in the three tongues you speak in your sleep:
Lashkar. Tandel. Jahaazi.

They crowd us into the damp, shallow cradle
they call the fo'c'sle. Silly name. *Phana*, we call it,
phana: the hood. The wide fan-spread hood
of this coiled sea-cobra we're sailing.

At the Belvedere

for Sandeep Parmar

The seaweed farmer from last evening
swung into the Belvedere again tonight,
this time asking for a Liverpool Gin
– citrus not watermelon, he specified
as he pulled the moonless key
to the alphabet lock
from his frayed trench pocket,
the hurricane lamps loud behind his glasses.
He dropped the key and a sand-crusted trowel
on the bar. His fingers had guttered out.
'Let's call it quits, shall we, mate?'
he nudged me. 'I give up. I don't know *what*
to call it, this mewling, this barking,
this mad overhead windwhack cackle of the gulls.'

Sycorax

Woke up trapped in a tree trunk,
speech slurred, though all I'd drunk
was berry-blood. It must have been the old man
with his cursed and cursing stick, which spanned
my rainbow-shored island in tight, cunning sweeps:
swamps, jungles, rivers all measured in leaps
and leached, cropped, dammed to suit his will,
the magus in his coracle, his eye fixed on the kill.
He has caged my bright-billed birds in new names,
mapped ash from his crucible across the flames
of my volcano, tamped it down. My skin is bark
on which his steaming slaves will carve his dark
memoirs of war. He will claim eternity as his own,
raise his monument on my stabbed muscles, my powdered bones.

A Constantly Unfinished Instrument

for Brian Eno

Begin with the creeper.
Follow its rustle
as it uncurls across brick, bark and thorn.

Go out in all weathers, craft a score
from the grunts and growls
that escape the world-beast in its sleep.

Stay the course until you've caught
the quick, true surge of the ocean
that's felt the fire harpoon pierce its hide:

until you've heard the ocean flail, lash and roar
through the creeper,
heard it again, and heard it right.

Night Sky and Counting

for Teju Cole

You are in the dark
      looking up at constellations and shooting stars
      finding traces of adobe roofs and walls
      at the eye's radium rim while grass
      tickles your back. You notice
      some celestial objects move faster than others
      sorting red shift from blue note
You are the samurai of wide open spaces
      they scan you in their eyes you're a ninja
      betrayed by body heat you're that grey-
      glowing-to-orange smear in minutes
      you could evaporate
      leaving heat shadow
      printed on the ground to mark the spot
You thought you *were the subject the locus of consciousness*
      when the shooting stars look down they see
      an object with eyes a moving threat
      under the black mirror at which you point
      to finger-link faint trails that might be a hunter
      his belt his faithful dogs or a raven a boar
      a river of eyes you have no cover
You are in the dark

Render

to provide a service, do [someone] a favour
to give, supply, make available for inspection
to submit an account or accounts
to deliver a judgement
to give up, surrender

to translate

>   to translate into form, give shape
>   to represent in a painting or motion capture
>   to perform a piece, animate a score

>   to create an image from binary code
>   to colour and shade that image
>   to make it solid

to melt fat down to clarify it

to hand [someone] over to [someone] in another country or
        territory
to extract protein, fat and other usable parts of a dead animal

the first coat of plaster applied to a brick or stone surface
before it's whitewashed

Pompeii Mural

the colours have sunk
         to evening whispers
the hours have spun out
        across the bowl in fine cracks
       these poems weren't written in my garden
       I'm driftwood in the wash of a winter sea
in the bowl a globe of honey gleams
        the age and shade of amber
brushed with mint leaves
         dark tides threaten my pages
         this storm could drown out my music
lost avatar of nectar
    the harbour I'm steering for is a reef
    land holds more terrors than the angry sea
       those dusty brown plums
    were gorgeous enough once
for senators to eat
    before the emperor's scouts
marked them for the picking

Fly Away, Swim Closer

for Sunil Gawde

The blind lamp is a promise of dawn.
Fly closer, scorch your wings with praise,
grow a skin of distrust.

Somewhere, an insect is drinking the tears of a sleepless bird.
Somewhere, a boy has wormed himself into the roaring jet
that will take him across ice and rain to heaven.

Somewhere, reporters are shrieking as elephants rampage
through cities that used to be grasslands, looking for home.
Light can stun you. Light can sting.

Fly away, swim closer.

Marine Drive

There's a colour whose name I've lost
to the ash fleece of cloud, the grackled light
of a monsoon sky seesawing in the gaze,
unframed, a trap for the sailboat wheeling in the bay:
this colour that hovers between tenses,
some call it violet, others squeeze their eyes shut
when it surges through slate-grey folds of water,
either not-yet or too-late, never tame at your heel.
But look, the rocks are coming into view,
dazed seals resurrected from the waves.
The tide's worked itself loose of the shore
and drifted out. There are no explanatory notes.
What's left behind is not the remainder.
There's a colour whose name I cannot speak.

Natural History

A history of mammoths
    salted away in warehouses
scrawled in chalk.

      sleep is a secret you once overheard

A history of rivers
    snaking down steep slopes
walled in glass.

      clay is a wisdom that leaves no fingerprints

A history of ballads
    that dolphins sang about horizons
broken by microphones.

      shale is a darkness you struggle to weigh

A history of drought,
    gulls circling above gaunt hills,
waiting for rain to wash the words away.

      words are rapids that drown us all

Passage

Ask him at four
      the con man with the fancy herb
whether the shirt will still fit
the grain still stream millward
the girl still hold her balance
on the fraying rope

How to hold and frame
      no, see see see
as if for the first time
the raw unpolished yellow skin
of the door the warm brick skin
of the terrace the downy cream floor

You must be alert
      to coffee stain and mosquito bite
red cloud of panic on the inner arm
the river's pulse beating in the brain
its gilded fish bursting the weir of sleep
source forgotten mouth unknown

upstream and downstream braided
      one current from which the wounded dolphin leaps

slipping from this skin of water to the next
finding balance on a wave
                              it's you and me both
asking who's really native in passage

The Refugee Pauses in Flight

for Nuruddin Farah

What should I call it, this number that has no name?

Countries are working hypotheses that sometimes fail.
I escape from mine, my wings of flame
doused, my route sketched in rumours,
an alphabet of stone and diesel
tapping at my ribs.

Invented reasons, found in a drawer of mislaid knives.

Never look back, not even at the veined marble columns,
the coiling creepers, the rusty sea gate, the orange tree:
all that you thought was you.
Even the briefest glance over the shoulder
could turn you to salt on a photograph.

Pick up the key ring, slowed by its bunch of yellowed date tags.

Where to draw the borders of the occupied city?
Across brain lobes that sleep while fingers twitch
in spasms? Across tents that shiver and capsize
on a frozen beach? Across graves
on which the wild basil has grown?

Living among strangers, he almost forgot the names of his gods.

Wound

The olive trees cast shadows sharp enough to wound. I scrubbed them off my sleeves with a wet cloth. Sat down on a bench and waited for my friends to arrive, the hours so many flat stones that I aimed at the skin of a stream, watching them skip and bounce and skip and bounce and not sink. All the way across the water.

The moon had wrecked itself on a reef of clouds before everyone showed up. Some of them were glowing with such excitement you'd think a miracle was about to happen. One or two backed away when they saw me at the table, like they'd catch an infection if they sat down next to me. He wasn't there yet. Did he really think we would all believe him? Did he think we would all just fall down on our knees and accept that he was the Master come back? Then there he stood, the oil lamps rising in his eyes, and speaking in the Master's voice, to be sure. But that wasn't proof enough. It could easily have been an actor's trick. The others seemed convinced. Or maybe they were all pretending, forming a hard, hand-linked chain of silence around him.

I was on my own, the only one in the room who had questions that called out to be answered. He saw me hesitate. *Come here*, he signed to me. Try me. There's only one way to make sure, I thought. I stood up. I wanted to root him in his thingness, grab the hem of his robe and test his muscles.

Or show the others he was just a tissue of time. I wasn't sure what he was but I was sure what

he wasn't. He was a vapour, the closer I got, a musk fragrance, then wild flowers, then a rank smell of horse. He had been, no longer was, said he was again – would he vanish, would he be again? I stepped up to him, meaning to part the folds before he could stop me, when he threw back his robe and, taking my wrist in a firm grip, straightened my index finger into a bodkin with his other hand and buried it, dirt under the nail and all, a few inches below his right nipple, in an open wound.

Or his twin?

You'll never know, he whispered in my ear, will you? You'll just have to find out how deep your own wound is. That's why I'm sending you away now, out of this room, out of this door, away from those who believed without checking, down to the harbour, to a gaunt ship that will catch the starburst of the whale's breath, that will take you to a coast where the sun will beat down on you for six months, stopping only to let the rain explode across the rows of coconut palms for the other six, filling the backwaters until they raise and carry your boat east as you sing your psalms, which fill the sky like slowly scattered birdsong, and build your temples on promontories of cloud, and wait for the spear to find you.

Redburn on Shore Leave

Liverpool, 1849

Wellingborough Redburn Esq., seaman on board the *Highlander*, merchantman out of New York City, otherwise 'Buttons', is granted shore leave in Liverpool. He exchanges pigpen duties for a brief period of liberty:

Among the ships lying in Prince's Dock,
>none interested me more than the *Irrawaddy*, of
>Bombay,
a 'country ship', the name
Europeans give to   the large native vessels of India.
Forty years ago, these merchantmen were nearly the largest in
   the world. They still
are larger than most.
>Built of teak, the oak of the East.

chait maase chunari rangaibe ho Raama

The *Irrawaddy* had just arrived from Hindostan with a cargo
   of cotton.
>She was manned by forty or fifty lascars, the native
>seamen of India,
who were governed by a countryman of higher caste.
>While his inferiors went about in strips of white linen,

this dignitary was arrayed in a red army coat,
                    brilliant with gold lace,
                    a cocked hat, and drawn sword.
But ~~the effect was spoiled by~~
        bare feet.

chait maase chunari rangaibe

His business
        flagellating the crew with the flat of his sabre:
            an exercise in which long practice
                had made him expert.
The poor fellows jumped away
            with the tackle rope   elastic as cats.

ho Raama

One Sunday I went aboard the *Irrawaddy*
                                    this Oriental usher
accosted me at the gangway, his sword at my throat
I gently pushed it aside, making a sign
        that my motives in paying a visit to the ship
were pacific
            He considerately let me pass

baajuband khul khul jaye

Strangely woody the smell
            of those dark-coloured timbers, odour heightened
by the *kayar* rigging

            The lascars   on the forecastle deck   among them
        Malays
Mahrattas Burmese Siamese Cingalese   seated round
'kids' of rice from which
they helped themselves with one hand   the other being
        reserved
for quite another purpose

khul khul jaye

They were chattering like magpies in Hindostanee, but I found
        several who could speak very good English.
        They were a small-limbed, wiry, tawny set:
            excellent seamen, though ill adapted
to northern voyaging.
        They told me seven of their number had died on the
        passage
        from Bombay   two or three after crossing the Tropic
        of Cancer.
The rest in the Channel, where the ship had been tossed about
        in violent seas, attended by cold rains.
Two more had been lost overboard from the flying jib-boom.

sainya ko le gaye

I was condoling with an English cabin boy
        on the loss of these poor fellows
he said   their own fault:
They never wear monkey-jackets   cling to their thin
        India robes
                        even in the bitterest weather.

He was a farmer and they
were so many sheep he'd lost on the mountain

sainya ko le gaye thanedar

The captain was   an Englishman.
The three mates, master and boatswain   were Englishmen.
Officers, they lived astern in the cabin
        every Sunday read the Church of England's prayers.
          At the other end of the ship, the ~~heathen~~
        prayed to their ~~false gods~~.
Christianity on the quarter-deck
~~pagan idolatry~~ on the fo'c'sle
               the *Irrawaddy* ploughed the sea

ras ke bhare tore nain

The ship was a book of symbols.
The fancy piece astern comprised, among other carved
    decorations,
a cross and a mitre.
Forward, on the bows, was a sort of devil:
        a dragon with a fiery red mouth and twitching tail.

saanvariya pankh ke upar

Cargo discharged, the lascars were set to 'stripping the ship':
sending down all her spars and ropes.
      She lay alongside of us,
            the Babel on board
              drowned our voices.

In nothing but their girdles,
the lascars hopped about, chattering like monkeys
showing much dexterity and seamanship.

kalam se likh doongi ras ke bhare tore nain

Every Sunday, crowds came down to the dock
to see this ship.
    Amusing to watch the old women with umbrellas
who stood on the quay staring at the lascars,
a species of wild animal at whom they might gaze
                    as at leopards in the zoo.

o bidesi sainya

One night   returning to the ship
        noticed a white figure squatting
outside the Dock Gate
                    one of the lascars smoking
as regulations prohibit this luxury on board his vessel
    Struck with the curious fashion of his pipe its odour I
    inquired
Joggerry he replied, a weed in place of tobacco

kalam se likh doongi

He spoke good English
I sat down by Dattabdool-mans
    So instructive his discourse
when we parted I had considerably added
to my stock of knowledge

Godsend a fellow like this
a man from the moon
What he says   a revelation
Crusoe himself
among the crowds of
mariners from all   the globe.

ab ke saavan ghar aa ja

But this is no place for all the subjects
upon which I and my lascar friend discoursed. I will only give
his account of teak and kayar,
concerning which I was curious.
The '*sagoon*', as he called the tree which produces the teak,
grows among the mountains of Malabar.
          Large quantities are sent to Bombay for shipbuilding.
          He also

rangaibe ho Raama

spoke of the '*sissor*', a wood that supplies
'shin-logs' or 'knees', crooked timbers in the country ships.
The sagoon grows immense, sometimes fifty feet of trunk,
          three feet through,
before a single bough is put forth. Its leaves
                              my lascar called
elephants' ears.

o bidesi sainya

The sagoon resists salt water, insect attacks. My lascar told me
the *Irrawaddy* was wholly built

by India's native shipwrights, who, he modestly asserted,
        surpassed European artisans.

pankh ke upar kalam se likh doongi

The rigging also of native manufacture: kayar
        now getting into use in England and America
                        ropes rigging mats rugs.
The kayar is made from the rind
of the coconut   soaked in water, beaten
with mallets   rubbed together into fibres

ho Raama saavan ghar aa ja

Dried in the sun   spun like hemp   the fibre
makes strong ropes   light durable   buoyant ropes
good for a ship's running rigging   cables and hawsers

baajuband khul khul jaye

But the kayar's elasticity ill fits it for a ship's
        shrouds and standing rigging.
The *Irrawaddy*'s shrouds were all kayar, the lascar told me.
    In two weeks, the *Irrawaddy* had her heavy Indian spars
replaced with Canadian pine,

                        her kayar shrouds with hemp.
She mustered her pagans   hoisted sail for London.

le gaye thanedar

Cargo and Ballast

i. m. Édouard Glissant (1928–2011)

Everything will be used against you.

Beginning with an overloaded square stern ship snatched from the enemy. Look at the name. Who'd believe it was called the *Care*? The ship goes off course and there's water water everywhere but no water for the goods in the hold.

No one can tell it better than you:

so many Gehennas two hundred crammed into a space that could
barely take seventy
                  vomit naked flesh swarming lice the dead slumped
                  and chained
to the living
            the dying crouched their shackle wounds festering
the swirling red of the deck the ramp
they climbed   *the black sun dipping*

you fell into the belly of the boat
the boat swallowed you the boat devoured you the boat that was
steered by the open skies and stars and fluent currents stopped your
mouth cut your tongue

Noah-boat Jonah-boat

this boat womb this boat abyss this boat pregnant with as many dead as living under sentence of death listing on this river with no banks river with no bends river flowing straight towards the sunset line

where no ancestor can follow no god can heal

The captain's seasick
                     and dying.
The mate's a safe pair of hands
                         but he's sulking.
Let the drunk passenger handle it. He was
    a slave-captain before. Leave it to him.

What shall we do with 'em?
Throw 'em in!

When the time comes.

*

Everything will be used against you.

Beginning with you.
They've got you down in numbers on a Bill of Lading:
height, weight, chest.
If you're healthy, the plantation.
If you're sick, the cutlass or the sharks.
You're cargo.

44

You could so easily
be ballast.

From chained march along the coast to barracoon
from shackle and rope to surgeon from Hell
    to Noah-boat Jonah-boat
    keel-haul and over-the-side boat
hung-by-the-ankle boat
splayed-on-the-deck boat
                       let us go boat

*

Everything will be used against you.

Beginning with justice.

You promised us insurance against 'all other Perils, Losses,
and Misfortunes'.
    These goods were going bad. They might have ruined the
quality of the rest.

*The slaves perished just as a Cargo of Goods perished and were
jettisoned for the greater good of the ship.*

And now abideth faith, hope, charity, these three;
but the greatest of these is charity.
I am become as sounding brass.
I speak with tongues.

*The jury had no doubt (though it shocks one very much) that
the Case of Slaves was the same as if Horses had been thrown*

overboard. The Question was, whether there was not an Absolute Necessity for throwing them overboard to save the rest. The Jury were of opinion there was.

Drownload! Let the ship liberate itself from drag, from all other Perils, Losses, and Misfortunes, and sail.

Did it rain?
We had no water for them they'd have died anyway so we gave
    them plenty of it
The slave-captain knew
                    We left it to him
Did it rain? When will it rain
                    on the Noah-boat the Jonah-boat?

When the time comes.

*

Everything will be used against you.

Beginning with nine knotted thongs of cotton cord.
The captain's daughter, the cat with nine claws.
Such welts.

You are the cost and the profit, the goods and the risk.
Horse latitudes, broken compass, crooked crew, stench from below decks, all worth it when we get you off this boat in one piece and on the block.

When the time comes.

*

Everything will be used against you.

Beginning with the abyss.

thing of breath and muscle
you swing
> *from the belly of the slave ship*
> *to the violet belly of the ocean*

you did not weave this sail you did not stitch this shroud
on this Noah-boat this Jonah-boat this giant stickleback
no anchor no anchorage
> pray for the life to come
> after the convoy of sharks

When the time comes.

*

Everything will be used against you.

Beginning with chalk, sulphur, ochre earth, jagged bamboo, ratooned cane, and the blades and axle shafts of words that were javelined at you and that you turned into birdcalls, passwords, anthems, spells.

original victim floating towards the sea's abysses you call to the spirits of so many who never came up from the hold from the stomach of the ocean to breathe the heavy air of Black River
you hear their voices echo in the voices of these islands

You wear betrayal like a matted skin. You wear betrayal like an armour. You wear betrayal like a brocade doublet. *Our boats are open*, you sing, *and we sail them for everyone.*

When the time comes.

Baldachin

i. m. Bruce Conner (1933–2008)

It's gonna rain It's gonna rain It's gonna rain noon's salt flare the tide roars out from where the ocean's sucked its breath in sharp and spat it out so wide the boom and every boat every corvette every frigate every destroyer is spinning out from where the shudder of foam is rising booming hurling itself across the fractured horizons these lines so flat so flat the sands sinking tide roars on tide **that baldachin of milk-white smoke** you can't hear the runes the gulls the curlews the propellors the countdown the levers pulled the buttons pressed there are no shores for the boats that are spinning out in every direction chased by bursting clouds the blinding ocean turns eyeward

*

You are the company the name is you poisoner you cannot pretend you cannot hide you cannot swim in these neon currents *I am become Death the destroyer of worlds* this ocean one open mouth swallowing islands this art of making things disappear in a glow that throbs in the eye that cannot sleep this frame that's come apart leached the colour from every drifting current this voice that shakes the continents no earthly thing trembles on its breath **this baldachin of milk-white smoke** has nothing to hide no crystal globe no night of mean knives no shallows no depths all ploughed bare all punctured all furrowed *It's gonna rain It's gonna rain It's gonna rain*

*

Stop for the gash in the water's white and trembling skin stop for the broken prism stop for the compass bird that's out of control and doesn't know where to point stop for the canoes wedged in the mouths of rivers stop for the traffic of dead fish and silenced pigeons stop for the wood fibre cowrie-shell stick maps of swell and wave crest stop for the eddy stop for the black hole untie the sticks lose the shells there are no islands there to map stop for the emperor's fleet dredged up from the ocean's floor stop for the gash in the water's white and trembling skin **a baldachin of milk-white smoke** watch for the boat that can knife the twitching tarp watch the rip lengthen in what was water and fade

*

Lord of lost perspectives,
                        this might be the wrong prayer:
Give me back the untroubled pleasures
                                of the sovereign eye.

Track your camera across
                    the last sand-bagged line of clouds.
                    The continents have escaped the net,
leaving an island of pearl-eyed gulls
and bomb-crater pools to keep its drifting tenancy.

Spell out a lease of hazy sand and churned riptide
          where the palms hold barbed souvenirs of rain
          and the children who pick shells and bomb casings
have no memory
and no sight.
That's all I can promise
                if I let you play
with the forest fire of the sovereign eye.

*

What would you cast: a spell or a stone?

What would you call for: splendour, catastrophe, or both?

*

Afterwards, the archipelago runs aground in bloated water,
the water burns our feet.

The ribs of caulked boats scattered high on the beach.
Spangled clouds dimming in a raw trench.
You hold out your hand. The tide's practising its roar.

*

Walk like a wave.
Without casting a shadow
on the surf, brace and reel in
the great horned fish

that has mocked and nothinged
our bait, has never been beached
on this narrow island
of what we know.

Highway Prayer

If you're writing a fresh anthem
for the one scorched island
marooned in cyclone country,
be sure to put in a line
about burnt tyres and sleeping dogs
and another line on the flags, curtains,
TV screens, more flags, all the shrouds
the islanders are hanging up
to protect themselves from the world.
They need a saviour.

That'll be the man in the red raincoat
falling through an open door.
An unseen hand stops him, props him up.
He blocks the door, a crucifix
barring the passage of time.
Time burns right through him.
He clutches at his burst stomach,
crouching on the sidewalk,
holding fast to the creased memory
of a river he once loved.

In him the shimmer is great,
greater than panic,
greater than the fear of flies,

of stakes, of exploding shells,
of ending up as roadkill.
Tongue-tied, he reads
this Rosetta of violence:
this highway across which
sirens call to knotted prophets,
Batmen to Jokers, Jets to Sharks.

Bless me ivories, the land pirate says
at last, shiver me timbers.
In this place that found me empty,
in this place that found me parched,
I am blood, I am grief,
I am the returning rocket,
I am contrary to the commonwealth.
Lord of the booming antlers
on a yellow signboard,
let go, he calls out, let go.

Craft me into this totality
that never closes.

II

POONA TRAFFIC SHOTS

Poona Traffic Shots

June 1991–July 2014

I.

No trench coat saves me from the scattershot rain
that pelts me as I ride pillion on a scooter
snarled in a spiral
nebula of traffic.
No helmet shields my head from the scattershot
rain as I wait my turn to be
gunned down by the militant amber
eye of the signal.
                  I lock my crosshairs on peepal trees
levered in the bricked-up windows
of haggard barracks that cancel out all impulse
to return volley.
              So renouncing
the counter-violence of bombing runs, a monk
on Ashoka's hyphenating missions,
I phrase my peace in tamarind seeds
and offer it to the peacocks and deer
painted on the loud wall of a park. And tabulate,
as I wait for green,
the rainfall per square inch of skin.

II.

Telegraph wires skittle wet pigeons, short-circuit
in puddled potholes.
The wheels churning below us blow up
on impact with cratered asphalt like the three worlds
on impact with Shiva's rage.
                                        We race, we skid, I almost rise
to heaven and am reborn
in two seconds with hair brushed the other way
in two seconds the bridge goes bifocal,
                                        a split
persona: one half windy upper road,
the other half pier. The river is pilloried
in red stocks of masonry, its arms and legs
double-jointed, blue.

Wool-proofed against the excesses of the rain god's bladder,
droves of lambs brim daily over the lip
of the broken bridge, led to sacrifice by an old man
shaking a withered flail and not
the harlequin piper of another town, another poem.
Their frisking is the dance before the dance
of the knives. They troop past the vultures of the Small
    Causes Court.

III.

The wall floats on the wind,
a snake god going home
on a ripple of news from a queen

delivered of child, an oracle's gift:
a prince of herons and tigers.
From my bus window, the athlete wall
seems almost to sprint as if from Marathon
to Athens it had to bear word of triumph,
then sink to its knees, dead.
The wall wears leopard skin for small warmth
in the rain outside my patch of sight.
One of its panels says in anaemic poster red:
AMOHOL.

        A sign pruned of President Bush[whack] doing
        his bit
for the oil companies – *you back my scratch,*
I'll back yours – and yet the logo
seems imported from a Midwestern freeway,
blown here perhaps by cosmic winds.
Or might it be an ad for ammunition perfected in the Balkans,
or some Asiatic derivative of nerve gas or defoliant?
A byproduct got upon the many-tongued She
of fire and skulls, nooses and broadswords,
by bald scientists behind steel-plated doors?
    Anagram, crossword clue,
       the sign mosaics in the shower.
The lustrum restores the real name:
A. MOHOL.

        Timed with dying bleats, the loose-scrawled motion
identifies a candidate for next month's election.
Such invariables as the returning officer's tent, the sack of flour,
the bottle of hooch and the quick boot for the press-ganged
    voters
dissolve in diesel smoke when the bus

booms past wall, past panel, past tea stall and trellis:
with a half-moon swipe of his wiper,
the driver abolishes the candidate
and like a dream of blue hills,
blue hills hit the windshield.

IV.

Everything I hear is a track on the fictioner's disc.
Everything I read is fury gift-wrapped in zinc.
Everything I dream is cement picked out in neon.
Everything I sing is about Babel and Zion.

The house with the squat chimney on the concrete plateau
is as abstract as it gets. Actually, it's an Assyrian bull
stamping his front paws in defiance of the distant hills.
And those hills are really an army of pyramids
in camouflage, on the march, no one the wiser,
and the spies in the sky who are running this show
are feline in their intrigue.
Look how they draggle the horizon until it bleeds
banners of saffron cloud.
Look how they wire the house-bull's horns
to blow up when the mobs cry foul.

But the house-bull, rampant, commands the sky's corrupt
and long-out-of-focus lens to adjust itself,
and snapping like a hangman at an inquisitor's frown,
the lens hones its blur to the commanded intensity of vision,
reducing every stray detail and whiff of desire

to a scar on the glass, a land fault, an opium dream.
Sprung back and thrown, the hills sag like jelly.

Everything I dream is about Babel and Zion.
Everything I sing is cement picked out in neon.
Everything I read is a track on the fictioner's disc.
Everything I hear is fury gift-wrapped in zinc.

V.

The kick-starter has whooping cough, won't purr.
        A dead crow's beak
points from the trash heap like the tip of a schooner
        sunk in a shallow bay, a bruise
at first only grazed, then scooped by nautical furies
        from the coast's offered skin.

The schooner's drowned mariners have been studded
        in the inverse sea that swims
in the fitful logbooks of wandering planets:
        they're sun and moon
locked in wary, trucial equinox.
        But on rain-veiled days

this shallow bay, though bandaged in cloud,
        allows the blood to run
freely, singing pomegranate tunes in hamlets
        cracking under hot-tipped spears.
Impaled, its guardian icon flails its arms,
        squinting against fate's stony winds

through emerald eyes. These are snatches of a district
    I've recorded. And don't miss the dancers
in the ten-act opera that I'll consecrate
    to the solstice
and to whatever gods have managed to survive
    the depletion of the ozone layer.

VI.

Chitale among his cycles sits,
a Peshwa in a yellow shirt.
Turbaned turkeys strut in a pavane
around the Library; above them, an old bat flits,
too old to pounce.
He tells himself the assorted rodents
nibbling at index and annotation
are simply not worth the lunge.
Yawning, he crowns Chitale's shed with himself.

Rounding the rusty cape of handlebars and mudguards
as the squall streaks out in lightning,
the ship that makes it to the gate shored up
with sandbags and breakwater tyres
is a girl in a black skirt.

VII.

At Khadki, a field of litmus lotuses
begins to blue in the alkali rain;
the Army trucks passing up and down
that bumpy, haemorrhaged section of road

are the imperially mute Chitale's
thoughts in camouflage.

Foghorns tear sometimes through the scarecrow trees,
shoving the bell-metal afternoon aside;
lorries pull up alongside coughing tractors
and ogres stick their caged heads out to ask
for directions, spraying a mist of pigeons
over startled cyclists.

A typist keys a message downstream, a whistle
answers him. Not far from the express tracks, on a siding,
soldiers have pitched their tents on the spine
of a goods train. It's a knobby plain they've come to,
these gunners who trundle across the country, going
wherever the gauge and fishplate take them.
Riveted to their compasses, rucksacks, mugs of coffee
spiked with rum at every station,
they stop in deserts and jungles, setting the time
by watches so disciplined their hands remain glued
at twelve. Their dreams smell of ghost towns
and echo with the chink of coins
dripping from a convoy rifled in the hills.
Wherever they go,
it is always midnight or noon.

VIII.

When Khadki was a base, the stationmaster complains,
everyone stopped here. Now the long-distance trains
zoom by without so much as a glance

at the semaphore's proffered teacup, the fence's
marigold garland.
The stationmaster and I trade metaphors,
work by barter.

But when the pylons by sheer instinct let the hawk plunge,
his wits on hold,
his wings like blades,
his descent timed to coincide
with the elections, when the orators ride in
on the clouds, and he must duck
to preserve his sanity,
his plunge belongs to both of us.

The wind's forgotten tongue, struck dumb
by speeches, wets a half-built house
from door-hole to gutted walls that have toppled
into haywire fields where a discoloured poster
still holds high the chalky name and ivory grin
of the Party's assassinated god.

His arm breaks the cordon of the poster,
offers the working classes a hand up
till the hawk snaps it off, sweeping it eastward.

IX.

In one lotus stalk out of a hundred in the field,
the king of the gods, Indra himself,
hides from a curse.
He lurks there, waiting in the pith for the black clouds

thrown up by the passing traffic to lift,
an atom ready to explode.

He has thought himself into a word
that I know this very moment
is swimming in the mouth of a fish:
it will come home in a catch, lie delicately
on my catalyst plate. I'll prong a forkful,
stand by for the shock wave in my throat.

The pen takes the page for its citadel, keeping out the dragons
at the edge of each sentence. The ink takes the shape
that the driving nib gives it,
as timber ashed by the passage of lightning
becomes the sky's voice among objects.

But when the bolt misses its mark, burying its charred code
in the wet earth outside the door, the rafters drop
a veil: sleep settles on the cat's fur,
a cinnamon sheen; a flute's high notes
hollow the lungs of the house, prickle the trestles
of tables, lull the black buck and the brocade girl
in the oval miniature to sleep.

The spines of books standing in rows,
the inner wheel of a shield embossed
with chinar leaves, and the wastes of Siberia
spun off a globe on an upper shelf have caught
the slanting edge of the light.
These sparks work themselves into my dreams.
Three dogs lick at lamplight in the hall.

X.

The electricity dead, by two candles
I think in longhand, typing as I do.
Like a Vermeer room, this room holds in measure
the evaporating light the sundial has notched up,
the glow that shifts from hour to hour on the white wall,
charting its orbit in the grain of the paint.
The shadow that stubbles the edge of the door
must be shaved.

The thin flame is my first witness:
reaching for torches
that toss like meteors on an idle breeze,
I carve shrewd emblems from rustling prayers
and seal the folded page by the formal light
of the thicker flame.

Wax on a word.
               A hissing idea
flickers on a jade bowl,
three porcelain crucibles
and the copper bodies of pens.
And like a withdrawn star
or fitful emphasis, a frosted bell jar
throbs with nimble, nervous lightning.
Through hard words and praise,
legends erased and rephrased in the dark,
they keep their secrets inviolate.

III

ARCHIPELAGO

Philip Guston, in (Pretty Much) His Own Words

A Triptych

1. Lecture

The hell with art, I said, and went through the mirror.
You couldn't catch me for two years.

The paw that drew the first line, that's what I was after.
Somewhere in Egypt or Ur. The *Ur*-line might have sprung

some magic grip over bison or deer. For here, for now,
you may want to take up these charred bones and follow.

So what else is there to work with? Black?
You can take it out with white.

Then you splash the mud over here. The window falls.
You can strap a wristwatch on that guy

who's got a little blood on his sleeve already.
So much you want to do with pencil and eraser

because you want to be spent, to finish and sleep well,
maybe even go to a movie. But finishing is death.

Which reminds me: Am I being paid for my silence?
I should remember that because everything I say is a concert.

2. Studio Visit

A book can become a tablet can become a stone.
    This lime skin is the binder.
But you want the name *and* the thing.
    And you want the movement.

This is about painting a book in the dark, to read
    when you walk blind into a curtained room.
Grab that paw and feel its pulpiness.
    It's not just a noun, not just recognition.

It's a lamp. It's a clock. Not just one brick on top of another.
    The process is a trial and plenty of error:
a ball and splinters of grainy wood lined up on a table
    and then some, and then some more.

When I get to the red head of that thing at the end
    of the line, it's going to feel like a trunk
and I'm going to want to pull it out,
    pull it longer and longer.

That's when they'll come and look at me in my cage,
    where I'm sitting and carving
a flecked rectangle of sky to look
    like a book.

All the anthropologists will be talking about
    this gorilla in a cage
and this gorilla in a cage won't get a chance
    to say anything.

3. Loft

Something gripped and bit at the canvas.
Did I really believe it? (Not: *Did I like it?*)
This paint didn't really feel like paint.
It spoke to me. I spoke to it.
Was it true or not, under the dirty skylights?

Taking no chances, I painted the whole loft:
easels, broken chairs, electrical wire
hanging down, all the way down
to my hand, below, painting it.
I had a hard time sleeping that night.

It briefed me on looking, reported its world:
that chair, this torn cloth, oh yeah, my broken mirror
in dirty greys, fleshy pinks, ochres.
That painting was as good as a Matisse.
When I woke up, I destroyed it.

Poussin's 'Landscape with a Man Killed by a Snake'

for Ruth Padel

Lying there. Just knotted and crushed
by speckled coils. A whistling snap and bite.
I could have sworn I saw him smile.
But wrong, that. That was only his last try,
a grabbed breath short

of shining back to a table's warmth,
the glow of fruit, his girl's toasted cheeks.
He's lying there and all the fishwife can do
is shrug her shoulders, throw up her hands:

This happens all the time, you know.
Got to go, they're bringing the catch in.
Watch out for the nets, the thickets, the pits.
Don't stumble around in the dark.
Don't ask for it.

Aperture

i. m. Diane Arbus (1923–1971)

What would the knife-grinder want
with a broken spoon and a pair of melons,
a Japanese bowl spangled with an iron glaze
and three dried lilies?

He's waiting for the little boy and girl
standing hand in hand
to cross the chalk line between kerb and street

and go off like rockets

while the barber stares, mouth open,
through his clean glass door, razor in hand,
a customer strapped in his chair.

The ibis-headed god in the Art Deco panel
above the knife-grinder's door is candid:
'When it's time,' he says, double-checking
the man's heartbeat, 'you gotta use the snake.'

Passepartout

Press quickly through doorways.
There's no telling what you might see
if you stop in your tracks to fix a frame
around a capuchin chopping a watermelon
on a plank laid across a trench.
His cleaver slices ribbons of air, flicks slivers
of wounded fruit into space with each stroke,
leaving the green skin stippled, naked, empty
on bleached wood.

Or you might happen on the pharaoh of no-moon nights
– ice-cold plums await the brush of his fingers,
neon oranges light up and dangle just out of his reach
and he could kill for them.
In the forest of saw-tooth shadows,
every deer knows his voice and tread.
You watch as he slides down stairways of water, yodelling,
a broken microphone in one hand, dripping sheets in the other.
He takes yesterday's tabloids for his score.

From under the keystone under which you've frozen,
you watch the capuchin grin and wave his cleaver
at the Rameses of the Salvation Army,
who's raising his microphone and not in benediction.
They lurch towards each other from opposite corners.

Walk on, tell no one what you've seen, you mutter,
but a crowd's gathering already to cheer them on.
You find your voice, you find you're the referee
by popular demand. They meet at the trench.

You're yelling for calm but who's listening?

Printer

Francesco Griffo, inventor of italics

Follow his shaking, roasted hand: he sets chisel against
    wooden edge,
points burin at plate, strikes lead against wedge, lays kern
    against grain,
and so through the night rams out the ringing cavalcade of
    words.
The ink rains down in neat lines, an orchard's planted on the
    sheet:
psalms, verses, prayers grow; he prunes them all with wayward
    grace.
The page burns bright, the typesetter's eyes grow rimmed with
    red
from staring at tight, infinitely small and mocking margins.
His reined lust explodes in hot metal, then fine brocade:
most mornings, he ends up drunk in a canal,
bruised from a brawl. One day he will swing
from a hangman's rope, singing to the last:

Yes, in three languages Yes, I announce, I declare, I proclaim it:
I was manic enough last night to smash through all the
    typefaces,
to drug every font, and now in my own sharply cut sans-serif,
I've slugged this by dimming candlelight for today's edition,

this crazed compositor's invocation
to a dawn that will break over Venice without his help:
Where I'm going, there's blazing horror and no gentle
    restoration,
pitch the only ink, flame the only imprint
and icy darkness my Lord High Censor.
Find harbours, all you galleys that sail out
of my mind's bedevilled press!

Glass

As a river traps the shadows of fish
          the mirror trawls its freight of daily acts
          that hover midstream, then quiver, flash,
plunge into sun-mottled depths:
bodies erased from a surface still rippling
          with the phosphor currents of their fins.

The mirror holds the combing of hair,
          a loosened strap, a blouse that fell
          from a shoulder at noon, a puckered mouth.
Faces that have faded, hands that have dulled:
hasped in the inch-depth of glass, they answer your questions
          with the fossil poise of fish bones laid out in a
          dry course.

Freshet-charged at summer's end, you dive and sift through
    what remains
          after the doing's done and, clasping your proof,
          break the river's glass. You wave it arm-high in
          the rain:
the hieroglyphs twitch, spark, blur in a sound that, *Fatalità!*,
    was falling
before you were born, before the sun had opened its third eye
          and left barges to rust on salt plains that used
          to be seas

– a sound louder than the memory of rushing water,
                    a drumming that beats and soaks and drains
                    the darting signs on which you've pinned
yesterday, tomorrow, up, down, strange, charm, beauty, truth,
faster than you could ever hope
                    to scan and set them in a flowchart of home.

Rothko

Shimmering through pillars of flame:
the zero field, a burning gate.

Tablets blurred by the haze:
not yet word, not heard,
not thunder-voiced law.

The eye, before sleep, had taloned
a long groove in the night sky.
The darkness closed every door
in eight directions. The ninth is dawn.

Now the horizon folds and twins itself:
saffron-scoured, scrolling westward
to seabirth. It sparks to flame,
spells out an arc of foam
across the ocean.

The eye opens wide
in the house of whispers,
the house of sand
where eagles' feathers swirl
in eddies, and the terse earth
empties its veins.

Hangman's Song

A tired man will hang at dawn
for hearing voices in his head.
Tomorrow's newspapers won't be read
and the Republic will sleep peacefully.

The Rottweilers have been taken off the leash,
they are nosing out children in the dark.
Tomorrow's joggers will stumble in the park
and the Republic will sleep peacefully.

A white crow settles on a branch
stripped of its leaves, which boys shred.
The flayed rain trees will soon be dead
and the Republic will sleep peacefully.

The lion's open mouth is foaming,
his keepers have foraged for flesh all night.
They will pile up their plunder at first light
and the Republic will sleep peacefully.

A man is horsewhipped for bringing the sky
into a cold room without after or before.
They will nail his shadow to the door
and the Republic will sleep peacefully.

A man swings
like a broken clapper in a bell.
The hangman knows all but cannot tell:
the Republic must sleep peacefully.

The Oracle Tree

The woman walked up to the oracle tree
and bled its bark for answers.
It's no use trying, said the tree.
They've tied me up with holy threads.
Roots burn through my shoes,
leaves cloud my eyes.
I'm not me. I'm
that man jogging along the promenade,
arms outspread,
scattering fistfuls of feathers
to the winds.

At Twenty Paces

You thought he was a rumour
when he first rolled into town
in his straw hat and red neckerchief,
whistling at the pigeons and handing out
bagatelles at the café for free.
Then one day you saw him staring straight at you
across the stoplight. You weren't going
to pass him in the street without speaking.
You waved out, said hello, crafted a smile.
He didn't wave back. Broken
pieces of sky for eyes.

Sniper's Drill

Depending on where you're crouching
you can parse the gaseous middle-aged man
as slumping over a newspaper in his stuffed armchair
or dancing on the roof in a mirror his grandfather saved
from a burning city whose streets were raked
by a rain of gunfire like this one.

Open for Business

Newspaper bunched in hand,
you're misting the door with Lysol,
wiping the glass panels in wide arcs.
But the man in the blue paisley bandana
who's whistling the opening bars
of '*Hanv saiba poltoddi voita*'
isn't planning to get scrubbed off the menu.
He's pushing through with a crate of eggs,
his hands itching for whisk and skillet,
the first Spanish omelette of the day.
He's a dancer sweet-talking the boatman
into getting her across the river.
You're a tightrope-walker with a limp, nursing
a sore throat. You spray the swinging air with soap.

Rain Dance

The dancer wilts,
       her early lessons in balance
            squandered.

          The first rains lift her spirits.
      Only much later, as she hears
the reassuring peal of thunder

and the sky empties out
       cloud by cloud,
            will it come to her:

          lightning travels faster.
     The news comes late,
the damage already done.

Figures on an Amphora

The girls of this town are dancing drunk
    in festive black on the minotaur's horns.
Their laughter garlands his thick neck
    and perfumes his scored, sweating hide.

Pierced by their supple pride,
    dragged in chains from his lightless maze,
seared by the baying crowd, the intended sacrifice
    shifts from hoof to spurred hoof:

he shakes his scarred bronze head
    to a tune from his calfhood no one else can hear.
When he opens his eyes, the song ends.
    His fists clench around its closing phrase.

The first dancer feints, pirouettes, leaps at him
    with a somersault: her palms strike air,
her feet find purchase
    on nothing, she shrieks as the sky

dodges her grip in the torchlight.
    The horned ghost doesn't miss a beat
as she slides off his oiled, glistening back
    and breaks under his dancing hooves.

Under the Tree of Tongues

there is no healing.

Eight Rules for Travellers to Thebes

Beware of babies left on hillsides with their feet pierced.

Don't fight with old men where three roads cross.

Don't marry a queen twice your age.

Don't ask oracles what they mean.

Leave fallen brooches alone.

Keep a list of sanctuaries handy.

Try not to answer riddles too quickly.

The sphinx keeps the hardest questions for the end.

Miniature Painting

the worshipper as lost cloud
                as woodpecker
                as five-crested tree
                as turmeric plume in the night sky
the god as spray of rose petals
        as parrot wings sparking against rock
        as the sea's voice at first light
the worshipper
                as leaf serrated by the shears of love
the god as spear point piercing the rainclouds
the god
        as half-moon and starburst
        as hermit lying on a deerskin at the river's edge
the god
        as pomegranate tree
the worshipper
                as its bending shadow
the worshipper
                as kneeling saint
the worshipper
                as runaway bride
the worshipper the god
                as any one thing of a thousand

that we are, were, might have been or be
from one to the other the eye darts
                              a one-legged man
struggling for balance

Glossa

the source is
>in the pause

the source is
>in the spring

the split wishbone
>twangs in your throat

the hunter's arrow
>shatters your heel

the avalanche wind
>whips the harp of shocked trees

the startled caribou pulse in waves
>through river and mist

the rain has drenched you
>no skin to hold the body in

you've found
>your tongue

Tree Line

i. m. Stan Brakhage (1933–2003)

tree rings
 an absent biography

 litmus of lost events

 a perch to gather
 the rain's drumbeats
 to begin again

a sentence in dusty green
snow sutra of chained wheels
   on the salt road
summer *japa* of crickets announcing
   a delay in nightfall
song snagged in a flayed tree
its words rustling in a fugitive wind

marking the quay
 from which the sun boat sails

to begin again
to lose your way

After the Story

i. m. Chandra Hoskote (1934–2015)

From the anthill came the voice

> Two white birds perched on a branch,
> one killed by a hunter's arrow.
> The first poem written in its blood:
> the mourning sage's sudden curse
> falls on the hunter's ear as verse.

From the anthill came the voice

> Prisoner on the island of his suspicions,
> alone under his white silk canopy,
> he murmurs the chants that his ageing priests
> heap on the fire sacrifice. Then from nowhere,
> two boys' voices, high flutes above the drone.
> Dropped masks, startled faces. The boys sing

From the anthill came the voice

> of the golden deer in the forest, the princess
> carried off by the demon chief, the war, the siege,
> the giant red monkey cartwheeling across the sky
> and burning the island fortress. When the war ends,

the prince fixes his wife's fourteen-year wait
with a cold stare and an ordeal by fire.
The fire plays honest witness.

From the anthill came the voice

But the prince cannot bridge
a distance greater than the stormy sea.
Doubt again for him, again exile for her,
love twisted and beaten on a washerman's stone.
At last she will have had enough of his tests:
she will ask the furrowed earth to swallow her.
He stands up shaking, his eyes opened wide
as his children sing to the king his own story.

The Bungalows of South Avenue

I'd followed a bus that called itself 'Destiny'
in large white capitals across its back windows
down a burning road in April.
                                    We passed a scrim,
its lush palm-beach sunset trapped in a haze
shimmering above the asphalt, then rolled to a stop
where workers had squatted for a quick lunch.
        A ladder leaned against the side of a house
I'd known as a child: cool mint verandahs,
lace blinds, iced tea. Now I ran my hand
along a buff wall rose bushes had once hidden
and looked up through the ladder's rungs
at a lump of coal flaring in a blue-grey spoon
bent over with the rough heat it held.
Sun in my eye, the roof a milk cloud
that had stopped in its tracks.
                                    This house
that had found me again, I thought, could do
with more than the sizzle of a welder's torch
stitching up an iron seam, the lick
of a painter's brush jabbing and nuzzling
at cracks in the plaster, more than cement seals
to patch cracked bricks behind the hibiscus.
                Might the spiral staircase
with its gnarled garlands of Art Deco leaves,

rusty, peeling off, have been trying to speak
to the men in their dusty overalls, its cadences
white noise lost below the gushing pump,
the whine of saws, the pounding of drills?
Logos before *topos*, the word pushes its abstract self
before whatever the eye can open: what words
could magic this place back to me?
           Might the beat of a deep-buried mineral heart
have faltered through flutes that no one could hear
above the squirrels chittering in the gulmohar,
the anvil fever of hammers? And my own ears,
stopped up against sirens but also the twanged salutes
of cotton-carders, the descants of street acrobats:
Had I heard nothing at all? Had I missed a step, or a fall?

Self-Portrait as Child in the Rain

shadows trapped in the door
rain tapping out a message on roof and branch

an ampersand of cloud

scared bird wet waiting for the others to catch up
at the finish line

Marcus Aurelius

Battle's end. The mare sags through the rain.
The emperor weighs nothing in the saddle.
The clear, unimpeded thought
is his torch and blade:
he scorches a way
through the forest
of corpses.

Planetarium

A stupa with the night sky trapped inside, growling.

Kushan Dawn Song

Water wails through the house of bone,
leaving trails of silt in my sleep.
The weight of crumbling hills heaves down the melt,
carrying the eddying tumult of war, festive cries
and forgotten shapes of heaven.

I wade through these Blakean torrents to meet my image:
my image meets me on the steppe. Lost twin, I thought
he'd be holding out a unicorn's horn. *Look,*
I've saved this for you. But no, instead,
a round red stone burns in his trembling palms.

Above him, cranes gather in a wheeling dance,
shuffling off the sins of antique winters:
a harvest of phantoms darkening the sky,
shot out from the veins of bursting rivers,
shaken from deep seedbeds of snow.

Set loose on the world, they wassail their hunting songs
far from their scorched pastures, in someone else's blood.
I look at my twin. The steppe shows in patches
through his skin. His eyes are gold, his sleeves
are dripping sand. I take the stone from his fading hands

and run.

Dunhuang

For years, nothing.
Then torrents of sand.
What could you chant
against the howling wind?
The caves swallowed themselves.
Centuries later, abbots would scan
the sky for flights of cranes
to lead them to the lost lake
they were trudging across.
Here and there, they'd find strips of silk,
bookmarks in the archive of the dunes,
as they stumbled away from their dromedaries,
holding their breath, saving their prayers
for the other, drifting, shipwrecked shore.

Bactrian Drachma

for Shailendra Bhandare,

On one side, a face that's been kissed, spat on, spun in bright air:
    basileos,
                tyrant mining dry valleys
                        far from Homer's wine-dark sea.
                        On the other,
                  rimmed by a halo of worn ass-lip script:
trātara,
a cave-born echo, never heard the same twice, never fully
    deciphered.

The Swimming Pool

You're dripping away, shedding water and scales
as you climb

out of the pool, giddy, gills wilting into lungs:
searing balloons

of trapped oxygen. The light and lyrical self
is burning up on re-entry.

Purged, it stumbles from a wet pelt
sloughed off on the floor.

*

Shavings of sky, sawn by the wind, drop on the water.
You flick away the light of unreported moons.

Never disturb dust, attachments or silences.
The handprint you left on the wall
when you came out of the pool
is drying in the noon-heat:

you're a thumb and a digit
away from extinction.

*

Noon-shards: a grey man's hacking at a block of ice
with a sickle. Leaves shimmer on the water

that flinches like the skin of a sleeping dog
when he trawls the tree-fall with a frayed net.

Your body is a gathering intensity of shadows
broken by a surge of glass.

Regent of vacancy, gather up the folded bathrobe
from the abandoned chair. Settle

under the deck umbrella
whose shadow has migrated across the pool.

*

He gives in by degrees
to the slurp and sluice.
Little deaths claim his time.

Now another he enters his mind, tissues, cells:
that he is plunging through the upside-down sky
to catch the diver's farewell, the lost pearl.

Centaur foundling, surviving twin: they wrote me
on the brittlest pages of the songbook.
I'm wearing this season for the last time:
for the last time this green shawl, these leaves twisted

to form a diadem. Next year he will return
as fire, gulls floating above his head.
His image will trail behind him
in a canal of shouts and whispers.

Thank you, he will say to the lifeguard,
That is not my skull you have there

in the raven's mask.

The Poet's Life

He married birdsong.
He sailed to the black island.
He survived gunshots.
He wore a sweatshirt under his linen jacket.
He talked to parrots in Greek.
He excavated lighthouses by night.
He asked to be paid in paper money.
He counted up the day's syllables before dinner.
He wished the balloons hovering above the docks were Chinese lanterns.
He called out to the spirits of drowned sailors.
He walked down to the sea with the town's fishermen.
He painted their grey nets in grainy gold on the beach.
He picked up ridged violet shells and blew wet sand from them.
He avoided striped red-and-white blinds on summer mornings.
He avoided the roasted façades of brick buildings on summer afternoons.
He noticed the oranges in the fruit stalls were shrinking.
He remembered in detail the railroad town where he was born.
He collected the rust and shadows that gather on ageing metal surfaces.
He licked his stamps himself, the envelopes addressed in green ink.

He glued the spout back on the broken chocolate teapot.
He opened the door to the deck and prayed the tree would
  burst with apples.

Notes

'Ocean'

The languages invoked in this poem – Konkani, Sabir, Aymara, Tulu, Jarawa, Krio and Tok Pisin – are all associated either with histories of cultural transfusion or with histories of geographical isolation and a consequent endangerment; with contact zones, littoral spaces and trade routes, or with remote highlands or islands. All of them have had to contend with the aggressive claims of modern languages imposed and promoted through official use by newly emergent state formations.

Konkani, an Indo-European language, and Tulu, a Dravidian language, are spoken on India's western coast, which has for millennia participated in the transregional circulations of the Indian Ocean. Sabir was the lingua franca of the Mediterranean's sailors, pirates, traders, soldiers and artisans from the eleventh to the nineteenth century: with its roots in Occitano-Romance and Northern Italian languages, it absorbed Spanish, Berber, Turkish and Arabic elements. Krio and Tok Pisin are both English-based Creoles spoken, respectively, in Sierra Leone and Papua New Guinea. Aymara is spoken by the indigenous Aymara people of the Andes, and is spread across Bolivia, Peru and Chile. Jarawa is the endangered language spoken by the eponymous indigenous group in the Andaman Islands.

*

'Spelling the Tide'

This poem is based on an event described by the American philosopher, inventor, entrepreneur, printer and statesman Benjamin Franklin in Part One of his *Autobiography* (1791). See Benjamin Franklin, *The Autobiography and Other Writings* (New York: Alfred A. Knopf/Everyman's Library, 2015), p. 25.

*

'The Heart Fixes on Nothing'

This poem is a translation of the Mughal emperor and poet Bahadur Shah Zafar's ghazals, '*Lagta nahi hai dil mera*'. As Bahadur Shah II (1775–1862), he was the last emperor of the Mughal dynasty, which was deposed in the aftermath of the Great Uprising against British colonial rule in 1857 and its bloody suppression the following year. Exiled to Rangoon, Burma (now Yangon, Myanmar), Bahadur Shah II was broken in spirit; his sons and grandsons had been murdered, his family scattered, and the glory of his dynasty reduced to ashes. In the circumstances, his *nom de plume*, Zafar ('the victorious' in Arabic) seems cruelly ironic; his late poems reflect the bleakness of his final years. For a sensitive and detailed contextual biography, see William Dalrymple,

The Last Mughal: The Fall of a Dynasty, Delhi 1857 (London: Vintage, 2006).

*

'Risk'

The first two lines of this poem are adapted from observations made by the Perso-Arab geographer and cosmographer Abu Yahya Zakariya al-Qazvini (1203–1283) in his treatise, *Kitab Aja'ib al-Makhluqat wa Gharaib al-Mawjudat* (Wonders of Creation and Marvels of Existence), whose oldest extant manuscript is dated 1280. The third line of the poem has been adapted from the legend appended to a fifteenth-century compass map of the polar seas; the fourth line is culled from Job 28:14. My source for these extracts is a page in a chapter largely comprising quotations identified as 'Fragments of Myth and Enlightenment' in Christoph Ransmayr, *The Terrors of Ice and Darkness* (trans. John E. Woods; London: HarperCollins/Paladin, 1992), p. 134.

*

'As It Emptieth It Selfe'

This poem takes, as its point of departure, the note to the copper engraving of a map of Bengal and parts of Odisha and Bihar, prepared by John Thornton (1641–1708) and Samuel Thornton (fl. 1703–1739), official hydrographers to the East India Company. This map bears the following title, rendered here in its original grammar, spelling, and punctuation: 'A

Mapp of the Greate River Ganges. As It Emptieth It Selfe into the Bay of Bengalla.'

Several editions of this map were produced between 1685 and 1711, which has been published, with an extended note, in Vivek Nanda and Alexander Johnson, *Cosmology to Cartography: A Cultural Journey of Indian Maps* (New Delhi: National Museum & Hyderabad: Kalakriti Archives, n. d. [2015]), pp. 106–109.

*

'Lascar'

The italicized lines in the first strophe of this poem incorporate or adapt passages from Arthur Conan Doyle's Sherlock Holmes story, 'The Man with the Twisted Lip'. See Conan Doyle, *Sherlock Holmes: The Complete Novels and Stories*, Volume I (New York: Bantam Classics, 1986), pp. 351–374.

The poem is woven around the colonial maritime history in which the 'lascar' (from the Persian root word *laskhar*, literally, 'army') was a key participant. It contains words for various ranks of sailor adapted into maritime English between the seventeenth and nineteenth centuries from Arabic, Konkani, Marathi and Malay, such as 'seacunny' (Arabic: *sukkan*, rudder), 'tindal' (Marathi: *tandel*, helmsman), 'syrang' (Marathi: *sarang*, coxswain) and 'topaze' (origin uncertain). The lascars would most likely have referred to themselves as *jahaazi* (from the Arabic *jahaaz*, 'ship').

For a contextualized glossary of Lashkari terms that have migrated into the English language, see the novelist and anthropologist Amitav Ghosh's scintillating *The Ibis*

Chrestomathy (http://www.amitavghosh.com/chrestomathy. html). For ongoing discussions related to this subject, see, also, his blog: http://amitavghosh.com/blog/ (accessed 23 March 2017).

*

'Sycorax'

Sycorax is Caliban's mother in Shakespeare's memorable late work, *The Tempest*. Described as a 'witch', she is said to have died before the events of the play; however, the consequences of her actions inform the narrative. In this poem, I take the liberty of assigning to Sycorax the fate to which she consigned the spirit Ariel: that of being trapped in a tree for eternity. In casting Prospero as the occupier of the island and Sycorax as its original inhabitant, I act on a contemporary critical reading of 'The Tempest' as an allegory of colonial expansion. See Ania Loomba's magisterial *Shakespeare, Race, and Colonialism* (Oxford: Oxford University Press, 2002).

*

'A Constantly Unfinished Instrument'

In an interview with Paul Morley for the *Guardian* (17 January 2010), the pioneering musician and cultural thinker Brian Eno observed: 'One of the important things about the synthesiser was that it came without any baggage. A piano comes with a whole history of music. There are all sorts of cultural conventions built into traditional instruments that

115

tell you where and when that instrument comes from. When you play an instrument that does not have any such historical background you are designing sound basically. You're designing a new instrument. That's what a synthesiser is essentially. It's a constantly unfinished instrument. You finish it when you tweak it, and play around with it, and decide how to use it. You can combine a number of cultural references into one new thing.' See: http://www.theguardian.com/music/2010/jan/17/brian-eno-interview-paul-morley (accessed 23 March 2017).

*

'Night Sky and Counting'

This poem was written in response to the writer, photographer and art historian Teju Cole's account of his experience of the artist Laura Poitras's work, 'Astro Noise' (Whitney Museum of American Art, 2016), in the course of a conversation at the Haus der Kulturen der Welt, Berlin, 2 May 2016.

*

'Pompeii Mural'

The passages in italics are adapted from Ovid's *Tristia*, Book I.XI. See Ovid, *Tristia & Ex Ponto* (trans. A L Wheeler; rev. G.P. Goold/Loeb Classical Library No: 151; Cambridge, MA: Harvard University Press, 1924).

*

'Wound'

The protagonist of this poem is St Thomas. The name *Thomas* represents the Koine, or Alexandrian Greek, dialect form of the Aramaic name *Tauma*, meaning 'twin'. The Gospel of John glosses it in formal Greek as *Didymos*. The name seems appropriate to the apostle who will forever be associated with his attitude of doubt towards the Resurrection – a doubt paradoxically born of his loyalty towards the living Jesus – and his empirical approach to what would become a *mysterium tremendum* of the Christian religious imagination. In Thomas, we see ourselves: creatures of schismatic consciousness twinned against ourselves, judging ourselves against hazily perceived *Doppelgänger*s, always wondering who we might actually be.

*

'Redburn on Shore Leave'

This poem is a palimpsest-like improvisation around Chapter 34: 'The *Irrawaddy*', of Herman Melville's *Redburn: His First Voyage* (1849). See Melville, *Redburn* (with an Introduction by Elizabeth Hardwick; New York: Modern Library Classics, 2002). The floating fragments of Hindustani that appear through the poem are *bandish*es, or compositions, from the repertory of Hindustani music. Several of these compositions are *thumri*s or *chaiti*s, traditionally sung by women. These genres, whose origins lie in domestic or 'folk' contexts, in cycles of seasonal celebration or the romantic and erotic lyrical experiments of *tawaif*s or courtesans, have been incorporated into the hierarchy of postcolonial Hindustani classical music under such patronizing and patriarchal rubrics as 'light classical' or 'semi-classical'. Expressive of female desire and political awareness, many of these compositions encode the absence or loss of lovers who have migrated to the city in search of work, been imprisoned by the colonial police, or been press-ganged into distant indentured labour in the Caribbean or the South Pacific. In the course of the poem, some of the bandish lines are broken up, recombined, or mixed.

*

'Cargo and Ballast'

Dedicated to the memory of the Martiniquais philosopher, poet and literary critic Édouard Glissant, this poem incorporates and improvises around passages from his memorable work, at once psycho-history of the Middle Passage, sociological inquiry, *ars poetica* and political manifesto, *Poetics of Relation* (trans. Betsy Wing; Ann Arbor: University of Michigan Press, 1997). The poem also includes material from the trial of the owners and crew of the slave ship *Zong* in the early 1780s, arising from the dispute between them and their insurers, who refused to pay them compensation for the slaves they had thrown overboard as 'perishable goods' in the days following 29 November 1781. The Atlantic slave trade did not recognize African slaves as human beings and regarded them as cargo; sick or dying slaves, as well as newborn children, were often thrown overboard by slavers. Business practice dictated that the ill be sacrificed so as not to infect the healthy; and, in any event, insurance could be collected on what was chillingly construed as reasonable losses.

Even within this inhuman system, the *Zong* massacre stood out for its barbarity and cynicism. The *Zong* had set sail from Accra to Jamaica on 18 August 1781 with 442 slaves on board, more than twice the number it could safely have transported. Towards the end of the voyage, the crew embarked on a desperate attempt to redress a crisis brought about by their navigational incompetence, myopic avarice and poor provisioning. Between 29 November and 22 December, when the ship made landfall in Jamaica, they threw overboard fifty-four women and children, and seventy-eight men; another ten men leaped overboard voluntarily, in an act of solidarity with those being murdered. The vessel's name perpetuated a ghastly irony: a scribal error in the owner's records had altered its original Dutch name, *Zorg*, meaning 'care', 'concern for one's fellow human beings'.

The *Zong* massacre inspired – or has been cited in – many works of art and literature. These include J.M.W. Turner's haunting and compelling painting, 'Slavers Throwing Overboard the Dead and Dying – Typhon (*sic*) Coming On (1840)', now in the collection of the Museum of Fine Arts, Boston, as well as the Caribbean-British poet David Dabydeen's book-length poem *Turner* (1994), M. NourbeSe Philip's *Zong!* (2008) and Claudia Rankine's *Citizen: An American Lyric* (2014).

*

'Baldachin'

This poem began as a response to the American artist Bruce Conner's masterwork, the thirty-six-minute black-and-white film, *Crossroads* (1976), with a soundtrack by Patrick Gleason and Terry Riley. *Crossroads* is a sophisticated composition that uses declassified footage of Operation Crossroads, the first two of the twenty-three nuclear weapons tests that the United States government would conduct at Bikini Atoll in the South Pacific Marshall Islands formation between 1946 and 1958. Conner, collaborating with Gleason and Riley, generates a profoundly unsettling atmosphere of slipping time and uncertain space. *Crossroads* draws us into a conflict between beauty and terror, catastrophe and magnificence, and was shown to admirable effect at the first large-scale survey of the artist's work, 'Bruce Conner: It's All True', organized by the Museum of Modern Art, New York, in 2016. For a detailed account and finely argued contextualization of this film, see William C. Wees, 'Representing the Unrepresentable: Bruce Conner's *Crossroads* and the Nuclear Sublime' (*INCITE: Journal of Experimental Media*, Issue No: 2, Spring–Fall 2010) at: http://www.incite-online.net/wees2.html (accessed 23 March 2017).

The poem also includes the trigger line of Steve Reich's 1965 work, 'It's Gonna Rain' (magnetic tape with phase shift, 17 minutes 50 seconds), a pioneering manifestation of minimalist music. This work uses two Wollensak tape recorders and deploys looping as well as the effect of phase shift, as the two recordings gradually fall out of, and eventually return to, sync. 'It's Gonna Rain' was conceived in the shadow of the Cuban Missile Crisis of 1962 and the eerie proximity of nuclear catastrophe. The source material for this work is the recording, with ambient sound, of an apocalyptic sermon by Brother Walter, a Pentecostal preacher addressing passers-by in San Francisco's Union Square in 1964. Beginning with the story of Noah and the Flood, Brother Walter predicts a dire end to decadent humankind. 'It's Gonna Rain' may be experienced online at: https://www.youtube.com/watch?v=vugqRAX7xQE (accessed 23 March 2017).

*

'Philip Guston, in (Pretty Much) His Own Words'

This poem incorporates a number of phrases and sentences from the presentations, informal talks, exchanges and occasional writings of the artist Philip Guston (1913–1980), culled from Guston, *Collected Writings, Lectures, and Conversations* (Clark Coolidge ed. with an Introduction by Dore Ashton; Berkeley/Los Angeles: University of California Press, 2011).

*

'Poussin's "Landscape with a Man Killed by a Snake"'

Nicolas Poussin's painting, 'Landscape with a Man Killed by a Snake' (probably 1648), hangs in the National Gallery, London (Inventory number: NG5763).

*

'Open for Business'

'*Hanv saiba poltoddi voita*' ('I'm going across the river'), a Konkani song indelibly associated with Goa, belongs to the genre of the *deknni*, a modern musical form that uses folk imagery and allusions. '*Hanv saiba*' was composed by the Goan musician Carlos Eugenio Ferreira (1860–1926) in the last decade of the nineteenth century. The protagonist of the song is a temple dancer who tries to convince a boatman to take her across a river, to where a wedding celebration is in progress, and where she wishes to perform. The riverine boundary is a coded reference to the continual shifting of the border between Portuguese-ruled Goa and the Hindu territories that neighboured it between the sixteenth and the eighteenth centuries, especially during the Old and the New Conquests. For people in Goa, this meant the division of families and communities, the fraying of older social relationships and the emergence of new solidarities.

*

'Bactrian Drachma'

Between the second century BC and the first century CE, a large swathe of northern and north-western India – the definition here includes parts of present-day Pakistan, Afghanistan and Central Asia – was ruled by a multitude of 'Indo-Greek' kingdoms. The rulers and populations of these kingdoms embodied a rich ethnic and cultural confluence of Indic, Greek, Persian, Central Asian and Chinese elements. Bactria extended across parts of today's Afghanistan, Uzbekistan and Tajikistan.

The religious systems, coinage and linguistic practice of these Indo-Greek kingdoms reflected their plural inheritance: many of their coins bore simultaneous Greek and Sanskrit inscriptions. In the poem, '*basileos*' or 'emperor' reflects the

Greek legacy, while '*trātara*' or 'saviour' reflects the Sanskrit. The 'ass-lip script', to which reference is made here, is Kharosthi, used in these regions during this period to write Sanskrit and Prakrit.

Acknowledgements

I would like to thank the editors and publishers of the following journals, anthologies and books in which a number of these poems were first published:

Almost Island, *BLink*, *Four Quarters*, *Indian Literature*, *Indian Quarterly*, *Poetry at Sangam*, *Poetry Wales*, *Indian Express: Eye*, *Sunflower Collective*, *3:AM*, *Schloss-Post* (Akademie Schloss Solitude), *Wild Court* (King's College, London) and *Wolf*;

The Two-Sided Lake: Scenarios, Storyboards and Sets from the Liverpool Biennial 2016 (Rosie Cooper, Sandeep Parmar and Dominic Willsdon eds.; Liverpool: Liverpool Biennial, 2016);

Between the Ticks of the Watch (Solveig Øvstebø and Karen Reimer eds.; Chicago: Renaissance Society, 2017);

Atul Dodiya and Ranjit Hoskote, *Pale Ancestors* (artist book; Bombay: Bodhi Art, 2008);

Sakti Burman and Ranjit Hoskote, *What's He Going to be Next?* (artist book; Bombay: Afterimage, 2016).

*

My thanks are due to the curators and organizers of the following festivals and platforms, where I have presented some of these poems:

The Kala Ghoda Festival, *Times of India* 'Fully Booked!', TATA Literature Live!, 'Poets Translating Poets' (Goethe-Institut/ Max Mueller Bhavan Bombay, 2016), the Renault Mumbai Poetry Festival 2017, Words Tell Stories, The Poetry Club and Cappuccino Readings, Bombay; the Goa Arts & Literature Festival, Dona Paula; the Singapore Writers Festival; and, in Spain, Enclave de Libros, Madrid; the Expoesia Poetry Festival, Soria; the Episcopio, Avila; and Casa Museo Antonio Machado, Segovia.

I would also like to thank Anupa Mehta, curator and writer, who invited me to participate in the exhibition, 'Liminal Space', a collateral event of the 3rd Kochi Muziris Biennale (The Mill Hall, Mattancherry: December 2016–February 2017). For this exhibition, I developed a text installation, 'Memoirs of the Jonahwhale', around some of the poems in this volume.

*

Very special thanks to:

Rajni George, my editor at Penguin Random House, for her deep belief in *Jonahwhale*, her championing of this project, her close and supportive engagement with the book during its preparation. Arpita Basu and Paloma Dutta, at Penguin Random House, for their gracious collegiality as they piloted this book to print; and Gunjan Ahlawat for a delightful exchange of thoughts and images while he designed the cover.

For their sustaining friendship, and for conversations and collaborations over the years: Ilija Trojanow in Vienna; Jerry Pinto, Arundhathi Subramaniam, Sampurna Chattarji, Kaiwan Mehta, Mustansir Dalvi and Jennifer Robertson in Bombay;

Jürgen Brôcan in Dortmund. For their friendship, and for the inspiring manner in which they have at crucial times helped me renew my poetic journey: Ruth Padel in London; Sandeep Parmar and James Byrne in Liverpool; Steven J. Fowler in London; George Szirtes in Norfolk; Douglas Messerli in Los Angeles; Paul Tan in Singapore. Friends and fellow travellers in Wales: Rhian Edwards for marvellous occasions of *jugalbandi* in Bombay, Newport, Bridgend and London; Eurig Salisbury in Aberystwyth for his wry wisdom and his deep knowledge of oral and scribal traditions.

For the magical experience of 'Walking Cities: India–Wales' (2014–2015) and Gelynion: Nikki Morgan and Ted Hodgkinson; and the sharers in the *claera*, Rhian Edwards, Eurig Salisbury, Nia Davies, Sampurna Chattarji, Jeet Thayil, Tishani Doshi, Jonathan Edwards and Joe Dunthorne.

For inviting me into Liverpool's architectures of epiphany: Sandeep Parmar and Emma Hayward at the University of Liverpool: Department of English/Centre for New and International Literature; Sally Tallant and Rosie Cooper at the Liverpool Biennial 2016. For my initiation into the Belvedere, and their memorable poetry and art: Robert Sheppard and Patricia Farrell in Liverpool.

In the fellowship of poetry, translation, and journeying across landscapes familiar and strange: Nikola Madzirov, Alvin Pang, Nuño Aguirre de Cárcer and Subhro Bandopadhyay.

At Akademie Schloss Solitude, Stuttgart, for their warmth, cheerfulness and generosity: Jean-Baptiste Joly, Kaiwan Mehta, Sophie-Charlotte Thieroff, Clara Herrmann, Angela Butterstein, Maren Pfeiffer and the stellar team at the Castle.

At the South Asia Program, Cornell University, Ithaca, New York: Anne Blackburn and Iftikhar Dadi, for their warm and gracious invitation to deliver the Tagore Lecture in Modern Indian Literature 2016 ('The Soloist Performs with an Orchestra of Events', 23 September 2016); and Bill Phelan, Daniel Bass and Bari Doeffinger, for their collegial support.

*

As always, I thank my family for being my first crucible of thoughts and images. My wife and comrade, Nancy Adajania, has been on board this project since it began to take shape; her responses and suggestions have been invaluable. Some of these poems have their ultimate origins in my father, Raghuvir Hoskote's stories, retellings of stories and labyrinthine collection of books. Without my mother, Chandra Hoskote's passionate literary commitments, her belief and active support, I would never have become a writer; Amma is no more with us, and *Jonahwhale* is dedicated to her memory.